ANCIENT ANIMALS
TERROR BIRD

Sarah L. Thomson
Illustrated by **Andrew Plant**

⌂ Charlesbridge

To all readers and lovers of "true books"—S. L. T.

For my father, who gave flight to my love of birds—A. P.

The terror bird featured in this book is *Kelenken guillermoi*, a seven-foot-tall predator that lived about fifteen million years ago.

Published by Charlesbridge
85 Main Street, Watertown, MA 02472
(617) 926-0329 • www.charlesbridge.com

Library of Congress Cataloging-in-Publication Data
Thomson, Sarah L.
    Ancient animals : terror bird / Sarah L. Thomson ; illustrated by Andrew Plant.
        p. cm.
    ISBN 978-1-58089-398-5 (reinforced for library use)
    ISBN 978-1-58089-399-2 (softcover)
    ISBN 978-1-60734-610-4 (ebook)
1. Phorusrhacidae—Juvenile literature. I. Plant, Andrew.
II. Title. III. Title: Terror bird.
QE872.G8T56 2013
568'.3—dc23   2012029366

Printed in Singapore
(hc) 10 9 8 7 6 5 4 3 2 1
(sc) 10 9 8 7 6 5 4 3 2 1

Illustrations done in acrylic gouache on acid-free cartridge paper
Display type set in Mindcrime AOE by Astigmatic
Text type set in Janson Text by Linotype
Color separations by KHL Chroma Graphics, Singapore
Printed and bound February 2013 by Imago in Singapore
Production supervision by Brian G. Walker
Designed by Martha MacLeod Sil

This is South America
fifteen million years ago.
Tall grass waved in the wind.

Or maybe the grass waved
because something was creeping
closer to its next meal.
A long neck reached up.
A huge head peered
out of the grass.
A terror bird was hunting.

The bird rushed
at its prey.
The prey ran for its life.
It was not fast enough.

Thoatherium

No terror birds are alive today.
But they lived on Earth
for about sixty million years.
There were many kinds
of terror birds.
The smallest was the size
of an eagle.
A large one could be
as tall as a basketball hoop.
It could swallow a dog
in one gulp.
No bird has ever been bigger.

Brontornis

Psilopterus

Most birds soar in the air.
Terror birds did not.
These heavy birds
had tiny wings.
They could not fly.
They did not need to.
Terror birds could run—
fast.

11

We know that terror birds
were hunters.
They had sharp, curved beaks.
Hunting birds today
have beaks like this.
Sharp, curved beaks are made
for biting, slicing,
and tearing meat.

Hunters must catch their meals.
A terror bird chased prey
on long, strong legs.
It could break bones
with one kick.
It could throw an animal
to the ground.
The heavy head swung down
like an axe.
The deadly beak
cut flesh and split bone.

Theosodon

Almost anything
that walked or ran
could be a terror bird's meal.
But no animal was
big enough
or fast enough
or fierce enough
to make a terror bird its prey.
A hunter like the terror bird
is called a top predator.

Astrapotherium

17

Today there are other top predators.

Wolves.

Tigers.

Great white sharks.

No animal hunts these hunters.

(Sometimes humans kill them,

but they are not killed for food.)

Top predators are important.

They kill some animals,

but they help others survive.

19

Terror birds hunted prey
that was sick or weak.
Strong and healthy
animals lived.
Terror birds killed animals
that ate plants.
Too many plant-eaters
would eat up too much food.
Then many animals might starve.
But this did not happen
when terror birds hunted.
They kept a balance
between food, predators, and prey.

Promegatherium

21

Terror birds were the top predators
in South America
for millions of years.
Then something changed.
A bridge of land grew
between South and North America.
Terror birds moved north
on this bridge.
Other predators used it
to move south.

Canis

23

Now terror birds had to
share their land
with wolves and saber-toothed cats.
Soon the birds died out.
They became extinct.
Maybe the new predators
killed the terror birds.
Maybe they ate their eggs.
Maybe they hunted their prey.

Canis

25

Maybe something else happened.
New mountains formed
as the land bridge rose.
The weather grew cool and dry.
Less rain fell.
Maybe terror birds
could not survive these changes.

Terror birds have been gone
for two and a half million years.
Today we can only find
fossils of their bones.
They were the only birds
ever to be top predators.
They were the biggest
meat-eating birds
that have lived on Earth.

29

There have been
other flightless birds
since the terror birds.
Some are alive today.
Others have become extinct.

Elephant bird
- 10 feet tall
- 1,000 pounds
- Madagascar
- Extinct sometime in the
  last 1,000 years

Moa
- 10 feet tall
- 550 pounds
- New Zealand
- Extinct in the 1800s

Ostrich
- 9 feet tall
- 330 pounds
- Africa
- The largest bird living today

Emu
- 5 feet tall
- 100 pounds
- Australia
- Emus can run up to 30 miles per hour

Common or southern cassowary
- 5 feet tall
- 128 pounds
- New Guinea
- Sharp claws can grow up to 4 inches long

Emperor penguin
- 4 feet tall
- 90 pounds
- Antarctica
- The world's largest penguin

More to Discover

Do you want to find out more about terror birds and other beasts of the prehistoric age? These books, videos, and websites are good places to start.

Books
Lindeen, Carol K. *Terror Bird*. Mankato, MN: Capstone Press, 2008.

Zabludoff, Marc. *Gastornis*. New York: Marshall Cavendish Benchmark, 2009.

Videos
Monsters Resurrected. "Episode 1: Terror Bird." Discovery Channel. Louisville, CO: Gaiam Americas, Inc., 2010.

Walking with Prehistoric Beasts. "Episode 1: New Dawn." BBC. Burbank, CA: Warner Home Video, 2002.

Prehistoric Predators, Season 1. "Episode 5: Terror Bird." National Geographic. Burbank, CA: Warner Home Video, 2007.

Websites
See how a terror bird bites.
http://www.msnbc.msn.com/id/21134540/vp/38745678#38745678

See a terror bird's skeleton.
http://www.fossil-treasures-of-florida.com/terror-bird.html